LEADERS IN MINISTRY & BUSINESS

This Is Our Time To Launch All Possibilities

DEBORAH FRANKLIN™ PUBLISHING
Your Story Has Purpose

DEBORAH FRANKLIN™
PUBLISHING
Your Story Has Purpose

Church Girl CEO Quarterly Journal

Welcome! Congratulations on getting your copy of the "Church Girl CEO Quarterly Journal". The purpose of the journal is to help you to write the vision, make it plain and execute. Utilizing this journal will assist you in planning and organizing your quarter. The journal is broken into five sections and aligns with the exercises in the book in more detail.

Scripture of The Week

Choose a scripture to meditate on for the week. This will assist in keeping the word relevant in your business and to motivate you while working on your projects.

Practice Gratitude

Positive energy creates positive energy. One of the key ways to experiencing peace and joy in your life is to practice gratitude. This section helps you to practice gratitude everyday even in those difficult times when finding things to be thankful for can be hard.

Prayers

In this section, you will write down and pray intentionally for what you want God to do or reveal to you for your business, personal and full of power.

Journal Entry

This section helps you identify and confront what you are truly looking for. You will take a deep dive into where you want your business to be extended to. This section assist in bringing clarity to how you want to enlarge your territory.

Visualize what you want

In this section you will create a vision and action plan for the woman you want to be. Your plans will assist you with identifying your purpose, visualizing what you want, setting goals, defining your why, and the actions require to manifest your vision.

The LORD replies,

"Write down the message I am giving you. Write it clearly on the tablets you use. Then a messenger can read it and run to announce it. The message I give you waits for the time I have appointed. It speaks about what is going to happen. And all of it will come true. It might take a while. But wait for it. You can be sure it will come. It will happen when

Habakkuk 2:2-3 NIRV

Sunday	Monday	Tuesday	Wednesday	Thursday	Friday	Saturday

DEBORAH FRANKLIN™
PUBLISHING
Your Story Has Purpose

Scripture of the Week

Psalms 23 (NIV)

1   The Lord is my shepherd, I lack nothing. 2 He makes me lie down in green pastures, he leads me beside quiet waters,

3   He refreshes my soul. He guides me along the right paths for his name's sake.

4   Even though I walk through the darkest valley,[a] I will fear no evil, for you are with me; your rod and your staff, they comfort me.

5   You prepare a table before me in the presence of my enemies. You anoint my head with oil; my cup overflows.

6   Surely your goodness and love will follow me all the days of my life, and I will dwell in the house of the Lord forever.

PLANNER
Make Today Count!

Today's Goals: `   To-Do List:

Reminders:

PLANNER

Make Today Count!

Today's Goals: To-Do List:

Reminders:

PLANNER

Make Today Count!

Today's Goals: **To-Do List:**

Reminders:

PLANNER

Make Today Count!

Today's Goals: To-Do List:

Reminders:

PLANNER

Make Today Count!

Today's Goals: `   To-Do List:

Reminders:

PLANNER

Make Today Count!

Today's Goals: To-Do List:

Reminders:

PLANNER

Make Today Count!

Today's Goals: To-Do List:

Reminders:

EVERY NO IS PREPARATION FOR YES!

KEEP MOVING CHURCH GIRL CEO'S
STRONG AND ON PURPOSE!!!

PLANNER

Make Today Count!

Today's Goals: `   To-Do List:

Reminders:

PLANNER

Make Today Count!

Today's Goals: `   To-Do List:

Reminders:

PLANNER

Make Today Count!

Today's Goals: To-Do List:

Reminders:

CG
CEO

PLANNER
Make Today Count!

Today's Goals:

To-Do List:

Reminders:

PLANNER

Make Today Count!

Today's Goals: `   To-Do List:

Reminders:

PLANNER

Make Today Count!

Today's Goals: To-Do List:

Reminders:

PLANNER

Make Today Count!

Today's Goals: `   To-Do List:

Reminders:

Scripture of the Week

1 Corinthians 2:9

But, as it is written, "What no eye has seen, nor ear heard, nor the heart of man imagined, what God has prepared for those who love him."

PLANNER

Make Today Count!

Today's Goals: To-Do List:

Reminders:

PLANNER

Make Today Count!

Today's Goals: `   To-Do List:

Reminders:

PLANNER

Make Today Count!

Today's Goals: To-Do List:

Reminders:

Reminders:

PLANNER

Make Today Count!

Today's Goals: `   To-Do List:

Reminders:

PLANNER
Make Today Count!

Today's Goals: `   To-Do List:

Reminders:

PLANNER
Make Today Count!

Today's Goals: ` To-Do List:

Reminders:

PLANNER

Make Today Count!

Today's Goals: To-Do List:

Reminders:

Scripture of the Week

2 Corinthians 4:18

As we look not to the things that are seen but to the things that are unseen. For the things that are seen are transient, but the things that are unseen are eternal.

PLANNER
Make Today Count!

Today's Goals: To-Do List:

Reminders:

PLANNER

Make Today Count!

Today's Goals: To-Do List:

Reminders:

PLANNER

Make Today Count!

Today's Goals: `   To-Do List:

Reminders:

PLANNER

Make Today Count!

Today's Goals: `   To-Do List:

Reminders:

PLANNER
Make Today Count!

Today's Goals:

To-Do List:

Reminders:

PLANNER

Make Today Count!

Today's Goals: `   To-Do List:

Reminders:

PLANNER

Make Today Count!

Today's Goals: To-Do List:

Reminders:

Scripture of the Week

Acts 1:8

> But you will receive power
> when the Holy Spirit has
> come upon you, and you will
> be my witnesses in
> Jerusalem and in all Judea
> and Samaria, and to the end
> of the earth."

PLANNER

Make Today Count!

Today's Goals: To-Do List:

Reminders:

PLANNER

Make Today Count!

Today's Goals:

To-Do List:

Reminders:

PLANNER

Make Today Count!

Today's Goals: ` To-Do List:

Reminders:

PLANNER

Make Today Count!

Today's Goals:

To-Do List:

Reminders:

PLANNER

Make Today Count!

Today's Goals: To-Do List:

Reminders:

PLANNER

Make Today Count!

Today's Goals: To-Do List:

Reminders:

PLANNER

Make Today Count!

Today's Goals: `   To-Do List:

Reminders:

Sunday	Monday	Tuesday	Wednesday	Thursday	Friday	Saturday

EXECUTE

EXECUTE

EXECUTE

1

PLANNER

Make Today Count!

Today's Goals: To-Do List:

Reminders:

PLANNER

Make Today Count!

Today's Goals:

To-Do List:

Reminders:

PLANNER

Make Today Count!

Today's Goals: `   To-Do List:

Reminders:

CG

PLANNER
Make Today Count!

Today's Goals: ` **To-Do List:**

Reminders:

PLANNER

Make Today Count!

Today's Goals:

To-Do List:

Reminders:

PLANNER

Make Today Count!

Today's Goals:

To-Do List:

Reminders:

PLANNER

Make Today Count!

Today's Goals: To-Do List:

Reminders:

Scripture of the Week

Hosea 14:9

> Whoever is wise, let him understand these things; Whoever is discerning, let him know them.
> For the ways of the Lord are right, And the righteous will walk in them,
> But transgressors will stumble in them.

PLANNER

Make Today Count!

Today's Goals: `   To-Do List:

Reminders:

PLANNER

Make Today Count!

Today's Goals:

To-Do List:

Reminders:

PLANNER

Make Today Count!

Today's Goals: `   To-Do List:

Reminders:

PLANNER

Make Today Count!

Today's Goals:

To-Do List:

Reminders:

PLANNER

Make Today Count!

Today's Goals:

To-Do List:

Reminders:

PLANNER

Make Today Count!

Today's Goals: To-Do List:

Reminders:

PLANNER
Make Today Count!

Today's Goals:　　　　　　　`　　　To-Do List:

Reminders:

Scripture of the Week

Obadiah 1:1

The vision of Obadiah. Thus says the Lord God concerning Edom: We have heard a report from the Lord, and a messenger has been sent among the nations: "Rise up! Let us rise against her for battle!"

PLANNER

Make Today Count!

Today's Goals: **To-Do List:**

Reminders:

PLANNER

Make Today Count!

Today's Goals:

To-Do List:

Reminders:

PLANNER

Make Today Count!

Today's Goals: To-Do List:

Reminders:

PLANNER

Make Today Count!

Today's Goals: To-Do List:

Reminders:

PLANNER

Make Today Count!

Today's Goals: `   To-Do List:

Reminders:

PLANNER

Make Today Count!

Today's Goals:

To-Do List:

Reminders:

PLANNER

Make Today Count!

Today's Goals: `   To-Do List:

Reminders:

Scripture of the Week

Joel 2:28

"And it shall come to pass afterward, that I will pour out my Spirit on all flesh; your sons and your daughters shall prophesy, your old men shall dream dreams, and your young men shall see visions."

PLANNER

Make Today Count!

Today's Goals: To-Do List:

Reminders:

PLANNER

Make Today Count!

Today's Goals: To-Do List:

Reminders:

PLANNER

Make Today Count!

Today's Goals: `   To-Do List:

Reminders:

PLANNER

Make Today Count!

Today's Goals: To-Do List:

Reminders:

PLANNER

Make Today Count!

Today's Goals: To-Do List:

Reminders:

PLANNER

Make Today Count!

Today's Goals: To-Do List:

Reminders:

PLANNER

Make Today Count!

Today's Goals: To-Do List:

Reminders:

Scripture of the Week

Proverbs 16:3

"Commit your work to the LORD, and your plans will be established."

PLANNER

Make Today Count!

Today's Goals: `   To-Do List:

Reminders:

PLANNER

Make Today Count!

Today's Goals: To-Do List:

Reminders:

PLANNER

Make Today Count!

Today's Goals: `   To-Do List:

Reminders:

PLANNER

Make Today Count!

Today's Goals:

To-Do List:

Reminders:

PLANNER

Make Today Count!

Today's Goals: To-Do List:

Reminders:

PLANNER

Make Today Count!

Today's Goals: To-Do List:

Reminders:

PLANNER

Make Today Count!

Today's Goals: `   To-Do List:

Reminders:

Monday

Tuesday

Wednesday

Thursday

Friday

Saturday

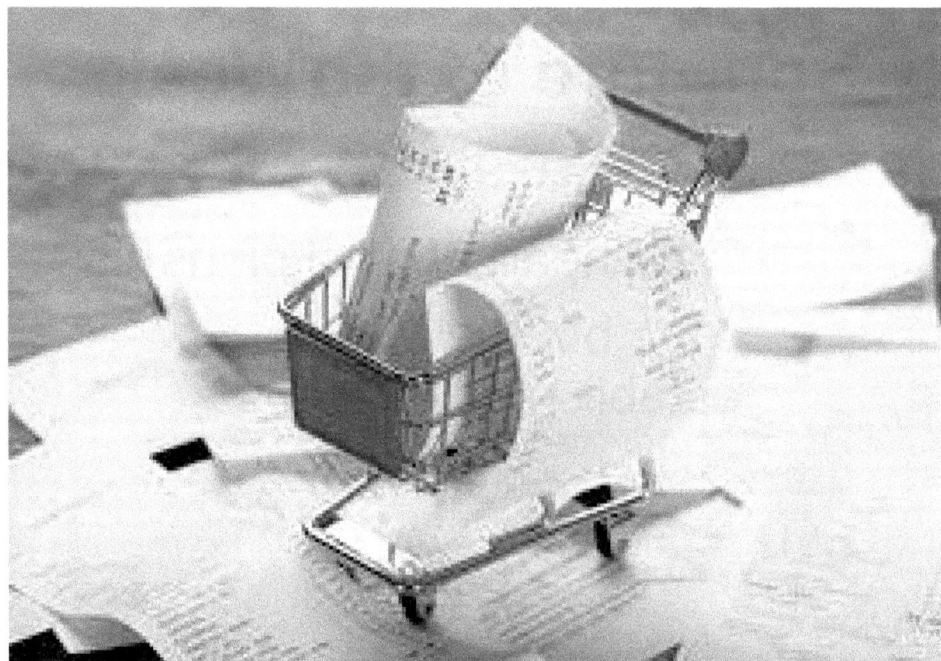

Get Your Receipts!!!!

You have been called and ordainedforsuchatimeas this. The power is in you now activate it!

Scripture of the Week

Proverbs 16:9

"The heart of man plans his way, but the LORD establishes his steps."

PLANNER
Make Today Count!

Today's Goals: `   **To-Do List:**

Reminders:

PLANNER

Make Today Count!

Today's Goals: `   To-Do List:

Reminders:

PLANNER

Make Today Count!

Today's Goals: To-Do List:

Reminders:

PLANNER

Make Today Count!

Today's Goals: To-Do List:

Reminders:

PLANNER

Make Today Count!

Today's Goals: To-Do List:

Reminders:

PLANNER

Make Today Count!

Today's Goals: To-Do List:

Reminders:

PLANNER

Make Today Count!

Today's Goals: To-Do List:

Reminders:

Scripture of the Week

Proverbs 19:21

"Many are the plans in the mind of a man, but it is the purpose of the LORD that will stand."

DEBORAH FRANKLIN™
PUBLISHING
Your Story Has Purpose

YOU ARE A LEADER

IN

MINISTRY AND BUSINESS

PLANNER

Make Today Count!

Today's Goals:

To-Do List:

Reminders:

PLANNER

Make Today Count!

Today's Goals: To-Do List:

Reminders:

PLANNER

Make Today Count!

Today's Goals: To-Do List:

Reminders:

PLANNER

Make Today Count!

Today's Goals: To-Do List:

Reminders:

PLANNER

Make Today Count!

Today's Goals:

To-Do List:

Reminders:

PLANNER

Make Today Count!

Today's Goals: To-Do List:

Reminders:

PLANNER

Make Today Count!

Today's Goals: To-Do List:

Reminders:

Scripture of the Week

Romans 12:2 ESV

Do not be conformed to this world, but be transformed by the renewal of your mind, that by testing you may discern what is the will of God, what is good and acceptable and perfect.

PLANNER

Make Today Count!

Today's Goals:

To-Do List:

Reminders:

PLANNER

Make Today Count!

Today's Goals: To-Do List:

Reminders:

PLANNER

Make Today Count!

Today's Goals:

To-Do List:

Reminders:

PLANNER

Make Today Count!

Today's Goals: To-Do List:

Reminders:

PLANNER

Make Today Count!

Today's Goals:

To-Do List:

Reminders:

PLANNER

Make Today Count!

Today's Goals:　　　　　　　　`　　To-Do List:

Reminders:

Reminders:

PLANNER

Make Today Count!

Today's Goals:

To-Do List:

Reminders:

Run
With It
Fearlessly

Scripture of the Week

PLANNER

Make Today Count!

Today's Goals:

To-Do List:

Reminders:

DEBORAH FRANKLIN™
PUBLISHING
Your Story Has Purpose

DEBORAH FRANKLIN™
PUBLISHING
Your Story Has Purpose

DEBORAH FRANKLIN™
PUBLISHING
Your Story Has Purpose

DEBORAH FRANKLIN™
PUBLISHING
Your Story Has Purpose

DEBORAH FRANKLIN™
PUBLISHING
Your Story Has Purpose

DEBORAH FRANKLIN™
PUBLISHING
Your Story Has Purpose

DEBORAH FRANKLIN™
PUBLISHING
Your Story Has Purpose

DEBORAH FRANKLIN™
PUBLISHING
Your Story Has Purpose

DEBORAH FRANKLIN™
PUBLISHING
Your Story Has Purpose

141

DEBORAH FRANKLIN™
PUBLISHING
Your Story Has Purpose

DEBORAH FRANKLIN™
PUBLISHING
Your Story Has Purpose

Your Story Has Purpose

DEBORAH FRANKLIN™
PUBLISHING
Your Story Has Purpose

DEBORAH FRANKLIN™
PUBLISHING
Your Story Has Purpose

DEBORAH FRANKLIN™
PUBLISHING
Your Story Has Purpose

DEBORAH FRANKLIN™
PUBLISHING
Your Story Has Purpose

DEBORAH FRANKLIN™
PUBLISHING
Your Story Has Purpose

DEBORAH FRANKLIN™
PUBLISHING
Your Story Has Purpose

154

DEBORAH FRANKLIN™
PUBLISHING
Your Story Has Purpose

DEBORAH FRANKLIN™
PUBLISHING
Your Story Has Purpose

DEBORAH FRANKLIN™
PUBLISHING
Your Story Has Purpose

DEBORAH FRANKLIN™
PUBLISHING
Your Story Has Purpose

DEBORAH FRANKLIN™
PUBLISHING
Your Story Has Purpose

DEBORAH FRANKLIN™
PUBLISHING
Your Story Has Purpose

DEBORAH FRANKLIN™
PUBLISHING
Your Story Has Purpose

DEBORAH FRANKLIN™
PUBLISHING
Your Story Has Purpose

DEBORAH FRANKLIN™
PUBLISHING
Your Story Has Purpose

Your Story Has Purpose

DEBORAH FRANKLIN™
PUBLISHING
Your Story Has Purpose

DEBORAH FRANKLIN™
PUBLISHING
Your Story Has Purpose

180

DEBORAH FRANKLIN™
PUBLISHING
Your Story Has Purpose

DEBORAH FRANKLIN™
PUBLISHING
Your Story Has Purpose

V

DEBORAH FRANKLIN™
PUBLISHING
Your Story Has Purpose

DEBORAH FRANKLIN™
PUBLISHING
Your Story Has Purpose

DEBORAH FRANKLIN™
PUBLISHING
Your Story Has Purpose

DEBORAH FRANKLIN™
PUBLISHING
Your Story Has Purpose

191

DEBORAH FRANKLIN™
PUBLISHING
Your Story Has Purpose

DEBORAH FRANKLIN™
PUBLISHING
Your Story Has Purpose

DEBORAH FRANKLIN™
PUBLISHING
Your Story Has Purpose

DEBORAH FRANKLIN™
PUBLISHING
Your Story Has Purpose

197

DEBORAH FRANKLIN™
PUBLISHING
Your Story Has Purpose

DEBORAH FRANKLIN™
PUBLISHING
Your Story Has Purpose

www.ingramcontent.com/pod-product-compliance
Lightning Source LLC
Chambersburg PA
CBHW051903090426

42811CB00003B/444